D1338003

THE
ANCIENT
GREEKS

Clare Oliver

p

CONTENTS

British Library Cataloguing-in-Publication Data

A catalogue record for this book is available from
the British Library.

ISBN 1-40540-961-4

Printed in Dubai

Designers
Julie Joubinaux, Rob Shone

Illustrator
Terry Riley (SGA)

Cartoonist
Peter Wilks (SGA)

Editor
James Pickering

THE GREEK WORLD
4

CITY STATES
6

SOLDIERS AND SNEAKS
8

BREAD, OLIVES AND WINE
10

DRESSING UP
12

HOME LIFE

14

CHILDHOOD DAYS

16

MASKS AND MUSIC

18

TELLING TALES

20

GROUCHY GODS

22

WAYS OF WORSHIP

24

SPORTING TIMES

26

GREAT GREEKS

28

END OF ANCIENT GREECE

30

INDEX

32

THE GREEK WORLD

THE ANCIENT GREEKS lived from around 1500 BC. At first, they lived on mainland Greece and its many islands – the lands that make up Greece today.

Greece is very hilly, so farmland was scarce, but the Greeks were brilliant boat-builders. They soon grew rich as traders. They built beautiful cities, trained brave armies and produced clever statesmen.

CAN YOU BELIEVE IT?
Ancient Greece was a single country.

NO. The Greeks swapped ideas and joined forces in a crisis. But really they lived in independent city states, cut off from each other by mountains or sea.

Merchant ships

The Greeks sailed around the Aegean Sea and beyond. They were perfectly placed to become the most important merchants in the ancient world. They traded goods from Europe, to the west, and Asia, to the east.

MAP OF THE GREEK HOMELAND

From around 750 BC, some Greeks left their homes in search of new ones. They set up trading posts and colonies along the coasts of the Mediterranean and Black Seas. By around 450 BC, Greek culture was flourishing on three continents – Europe, Asia and Africa.

Greek colonies

EUROPE

Greek homelands

Black Sea

ASIA

Mediterranean Sea

AFRICA

YOU MUST BE JOKING!

Greek settlers in southern Italy led a life of amazing luxury. They were said to sleep each night on beds of fresh, sweet-smelling rose petals!

CITY STATES

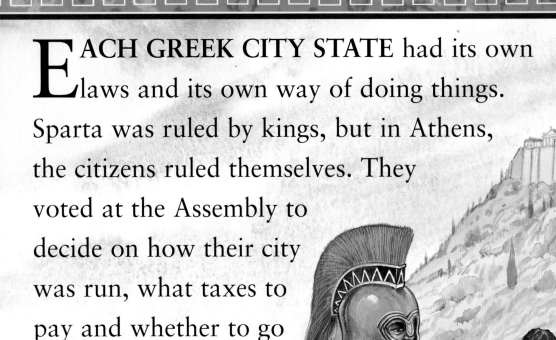

EACH GREEK CITY STATE had its own laws and its own way of doing things. Sparta was ruled by kings, but in Athens, the citizens ruled themselves. They voted at the Assembly to decide on how their city was run, what taxes to pay and whether to go to war.

YOU MUST BE JOKING!
The Greeks invented a water clock that timed speeches made at the Assembly. It stopped speakers from going on too long because when the water ran out, they had to shut up!

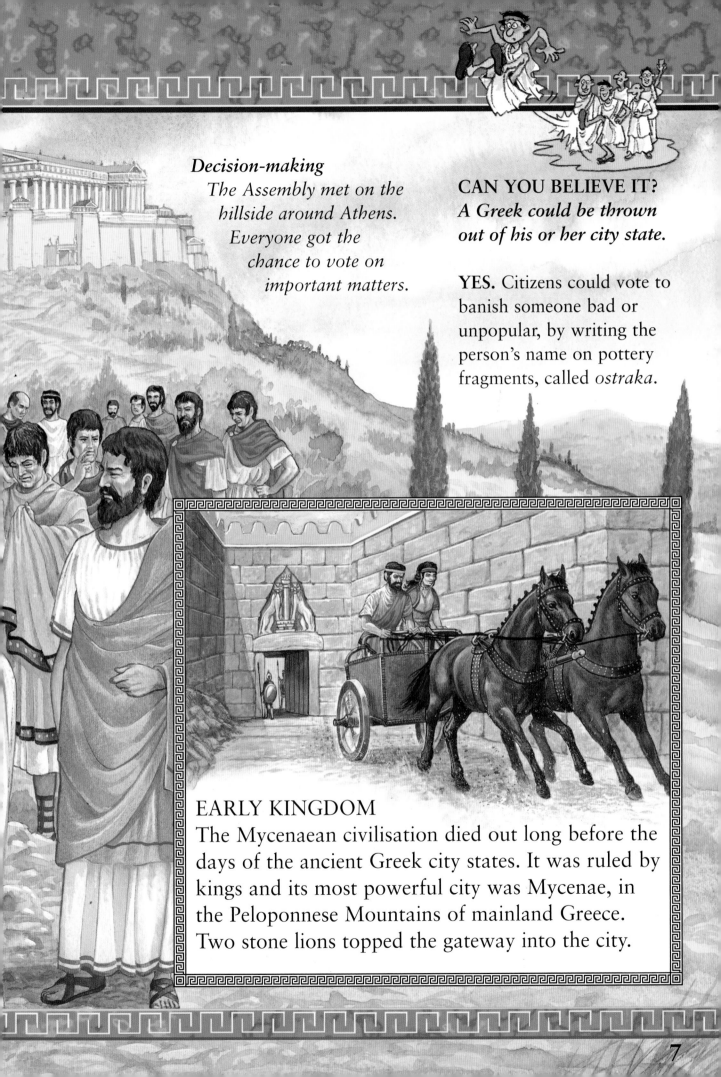

Decision-making
The Assembly met on the hillside around Athens. Everyone got the chance to vote on important matters.

CAN YOU BELIEVE IT?
A Greek could be thrown out of his or her city state.

YES. Citizens could vote to banish someone bad or unpopular, by writing the person's name on pottery fragments, called *ostraka*.

EARLY KINGDOM
The Mycenaean civilisation died out long before the days of the ancient Greek city states. It was ruled by kings and its most powerful city was Mycenae, in the Peloponnese Mountains of mainland Greece. Two stone lions topped the gateway into the city.

SOLDIERS AND SNEAKS

THE ANCIENT GREEKS were always waging war. In 479 BC, the Athenian navy saw off the mighty Persian fleet – but only after their city had been burnt to the ground.

Most wars, though, were between the city states. During the 400s BC, Athens and Sparta battled for control of the whole of Greece. They spent over 40 years fighting each other!

CAN YOU BELIEVE IT?
Greek soldiers had to buy their own armour.

YES. And their own weapons, too. Only the richest soldiers could afford to buy the right kit!

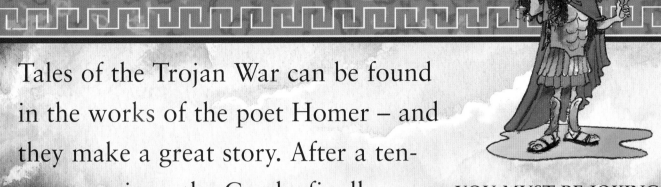

Tales of the Trojan War can be found in the works of the poet Homer – and they make a great story. After a ten-year siege, the Greeks finally tricked their way to victory.

Horsey hiding place
Greek soldiers sneaked into Troy hidden inside a huge wooden horse. The Trojans had thought the horse was a gift and wheeled it into their city.

YOU MUST BE JOKING!
Spartan soldiers did their hair before a battle. The Spartans were the fiercest ancient Greek soldiers. They took great pride in their long hair and beards – that's why cowardly soldiers had half of their head shaved!

GREEK TRIREME
Greek warships were fitted with battering rams – long, pointy spikes that stuck out from the prow. In a sea battle, Greek oarsmen rowed at top speed, straight at the enemy ship. The aim was for their ram to smash a hole in the enemy's hull, and sink the ship.

BREAKFAST IN ANCIENT Greece was usually bread soaked in wine. There was more bread to go with the main afternoon meal – and more wine, too! Wine was the Greeks' favourite drink.

CAN YOU BELIEVE IT?
At parties, the Greeks threw away their wine.

YES. Kottabos was the name of a game the Greeks liked to play. You had to flick the dregs from the bottom of your wine cup.

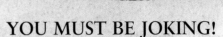

The Greek diet was very healthy, though, with lots of olive oil, fruit and vegetables, pulses and seafood. Favourite fish included tuna, sea bass and conger eel. Meat didn't keep long in the heat, so it was served only at feasts.

YOU MUST BE JOKING!
Only men were invited to Greek dinner parties. Their wives had to stay at home. But there were some women at the party – slave girls! They played music and danced to entertain the guests.

Chickens for wine
The Greeks had coins, but they didn't always use them to buy and sell. Sometimes they bartered, or swapped, their produce instead.

THE OLIVE HARVEST
There were olive groves all over ancient Greece. To harvest the fruits, farmers hit the trees with sticks until the olives fell to the ground.
Olives gave the Greeks precious oil, which could be used for cooking or burnt in lamps.

REEK CLOTHES WERE beautifully comfortable to wear. Everyone wore a simple tunic called a chiton, gathered at the waist with a belt or two. Pins held it in place at the shoulders. Women wore their chitons long, while tunics for men and children stopped at the knee.

TAKING A BATH

Baths were a luxury in ancient Greece, because there was no running water, but the rich had slaves to fill their tubs. Both men and women used olive oil perfumed with spices or flowers to moisturise their skin – and keep it smelling sweet between washes!

People usually went barefoot indoors, but they put on leather sandals when they went out. Depending on the weather, Greeks might wear woollen cloaks over their chitons or hats to shade them from the sun.

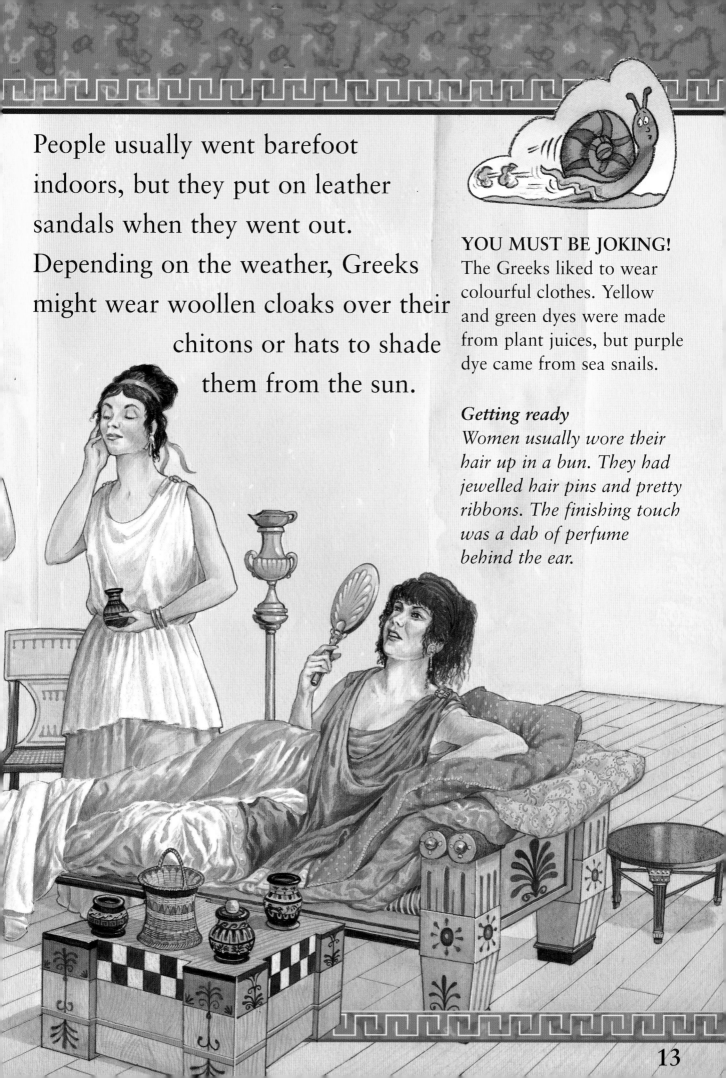

YOU MUST BE JOKING!
The Greeks liked to wear colourful clothes. Yellow and green dyes were made from plant juices, but purple dye came from sea snails.

Getting ready
Women usually wore their hair up in a bun. They had jewelled hair pins and pretty ribbons. The finishing touch was a dab of perfume behind the ear.

HOME LIFE

GREEK HOMES WERE built from simple mud bricks. They were whitewashed to reflect the heat and to stop the bricks crumbling in the sun. There were few windows, so houses must have been beautifully cool.

Meals were cooked in the kitchen or courtyard, over a portable hearth like a barbecue. There were no cupboards, so belongings and food were stored in wooden chests or terracotta jars.

YOU MUST BE JOKING!
In ancient Greece, burglars broke in through the walls! The windows were so high up that robbers preferred to hack a hole in the bricks!

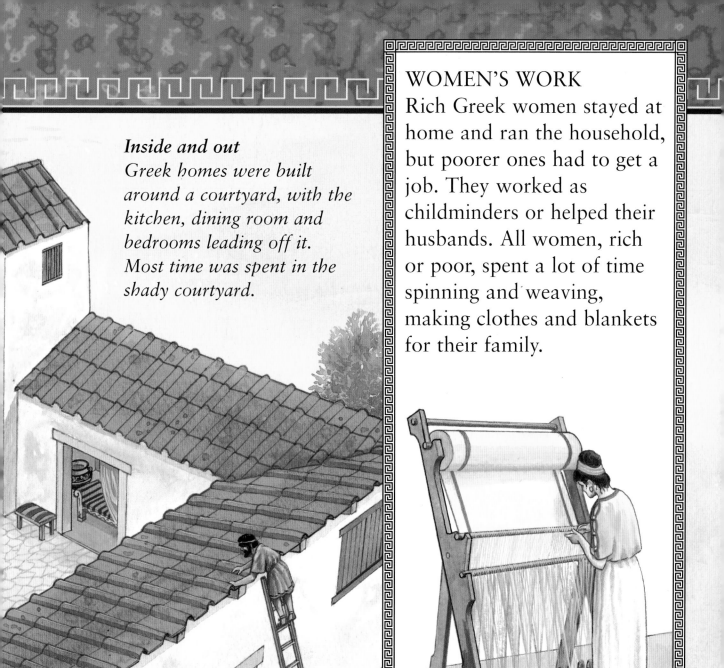

Inside and out
Greek homes were built around a courtyard, with the kitchen, dining room and bedrooms leading off it. Most time was spent in the shady courtyard.

WOMEN'S WORK
Rich Greek women stayed at home and ran the household, but poorer ones had to get a job. They worked as childminders or helped their husbands. All women, rich or poor, spent a lot of time spinning and weaving, making clothes and blankets for their family.

CAN YOU BELIEVE IT?
The Greeks had running water.

NO. Slaves had to go to the well and collect water in large, clay jars.

CHILDHOOD DAYS

GREEK BOYS WENT TO SCHOOL from the age of seven. As well as reading, writing and maths, they had classes in singing and making speeches. Games lessons were important too. Wrestling and athletics kept boys fit, healthy – and ready to be strong soldiers when they grew up.

Girls didn't go to school. They stayed at home and learnt how to spin, weave and keep house. Only a few girls from rich families learnt to read and write.

Age of learning
Boys wrote their lessons on wax tablets, scratching in the letters with a pointed stylus made of metal or bone.

CAN YOU BELIEVE IT?
Greek fathers preferred sons to daughters.

YES. When boys grew up they worked and earned money for the family. Girls would need a dowry, a gift of money for her husband when she married.

YOU MUST BE JOKING!

Ancient Greek babies had potties – and bottles, too! Baby bottles were made of clay. They looked a bit like oil lamps, and were fitted with a leather teat.

ANCIENT PLAYTHINGS

Greek children played with dolls and toy soldiers, spinning tops and board games. But they gave up their toys when childhood was over. Boys' toys were dedicated to the god Apollo and girls offered theirs to Artemis.

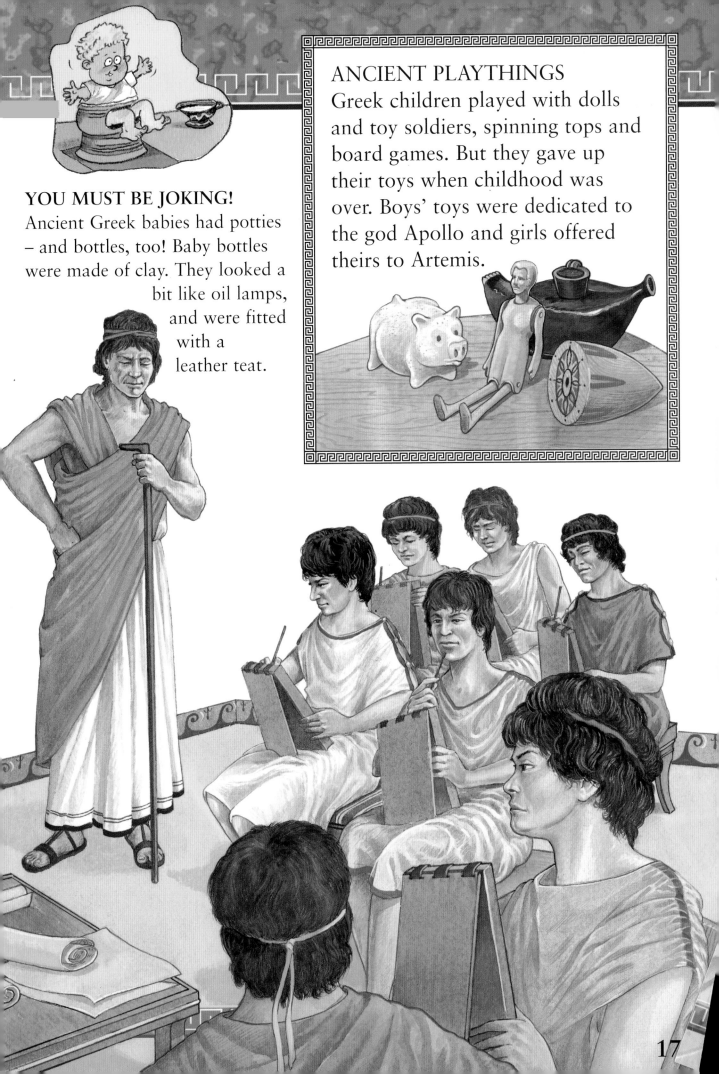

MASKS AND MUSIC

IN ANCIENT GREEK TIMES, plays were put on in huge, open-air theatres. There were two types of play. Serious stories about the gods, war and love were known as tragedies. Comedies were light-hearted and made fun of people or ideas. Plays written by the Greeks are still performed today.

Masked men
Actors wore special masks that helped their voices to carry.
The masks also showed what part the actor was playing.

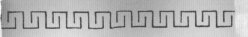

CAN YOU BELIEVE IT?
Some Greek plays went on all day long.

YES. People took cushions and blankets so they would be comfy and cosy. They also took along a picnic in case they got hungry!

Sometimes, musicians added extra atmosphere to the drama with cymbal clashes or haunting flute melodies. Music was part of religious festivals, too.

YOU MUST BE JOKING!
The Greeks believed that the same god looked after drama and wine. This god, Dionysos, must have liked having a good time! The very first plays were put on in his honour.

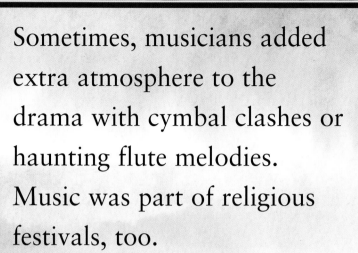

MUSICAL INSTRUMENTS
The main string instruments were the harp and the lyre, which was made from a tortoise shell. Wind instruments included the double flute and the panpipes. Cymbals and drums were popular too.

TELLING TALES

THE MOST POPULAR PASTIME in ancient Greece was telling stories. The Greeks made up lots of exciting tales about the gods, and about heroes who defeated magical monsters.

At first, Greek myths were passed on by word of mouth. Later, they were written down by poets such as Hesiod and playwrights such as Euripides.

YOU MUST BE JOKING!
As a baby, the hero Achilles was dipped in the magical River Styx. This made his body invincible – apart from the bit his mum was holding. That's why Achilles's heel was his one weak spot.

Monster Minotaur
The Minotaur was a hideous, hungry monster that lived on Crete. Each year, young people were sent into its maze as food. Finally, a brave prince called Theseus slayed the beast.

HOMER'S HERO

The poet Homer described the adventures of Odysseus, a king on his way home from the Trojan War. A one-eyed giant trapped the king and his men in a cave. Even after Odysseus had blinded the Cyclops, it still guarded the cave entrance. The men escaped by clinging to the bellies of the giant's sheep. Hearing the noise, the giant grasped around – but all he could feel were the sheep's woolly backs!

CAN YOU BELIEVE IT?
The Argonauts were scary monsters.

NO. They were the crew of the *Argos*, the ship that took the Greek hero Jason on his quest to find the Golden Fleece.

GROUCHY GODS

THE ANCIENT Greeks worshipped many gods and goddesses. Most of their gods looked like ordinary people – and had ordinary, human faults like being jealous or cross!

Greece's tallest mountain, Olympus was the home of twelve of the main gods, but not Poseidon and Hades. Poseidon lived in the sea and Hades, in the Underworld.

1 Apollo, god of hunting and healing
2 Poseidon, god of the sea
3 Hermes, messenger of the gods
4 Dionysos, god of wine
5 Demeter, goddess of corn

CAN YOU BELIEVE IT?
All the Greek gods looked just like humans.

NO. Most did, but not all. Pan, god of the woods, had the horns and legs of a goat!

6 Ares, god of war
7 Hades and Persephone, god and goddess of death
8 Hephaestos, god of fire and metalwork
9 Artemis, goddess of hunting
10 Aphrodite, goddess of love
11 Hera, queen of the gods
12 Athene, goddess of war
13 Hestia, goddess of hearth and home
14 Zeus, king of the gods

YOU MUST BE JOKING!

Cronos was king before Zeus. So he could stay king, he gobbled up most of his children. Luckily, Zeus's mum tricked Cronos into eating a stone instead of the baby!

GODDESS OF ATHENS

The war goddess Athene was also the protector of Athens. A beautiful temple called the Parthenon was built in her honour. Inside, priests made offerings to a beautiful gold and ivory statue of the goddess.

WAYS OF WORSHIP

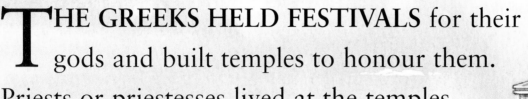

THE GREEKS HELD FESTIVALS for their gods and built temples to honour them. Priests or priestesses lived at the temples and performed special rituals each day.

Offerings were an important part of Greek worship. The Greeks didn't want to anger the gods, so they always washed and made an offering of food or wine before they started praying.

CAN YOU BELIEVE IT?
People offered up statues of their feet to a god.

YES. People took model feet or other body parts to the shrine of Aesclepius. They hoped he would heal them.

Gifts for a god
At festival time, people took offerings to the temple – olive oil, wine and livestock. They even brought clothes for the temple statues of the god to wear!

THE ORACLE AT DELPHI

The Greeks asked the gods before they did anything. Many went to Apollo's shrine at Delphi to ask advice. A priestess called the Pythia would go into a trance to find out Apollo's answer. Her words sounded like gobbledegook – but the priests could interpret them.

YOU MUST BE JOKING!

The Greeks believed they went to the Underworld when they died. First, though, they had to cross the River Styx. So the dead were buried with a coin in their mouths – to pay the ferry fare!

SPORTING TIMES

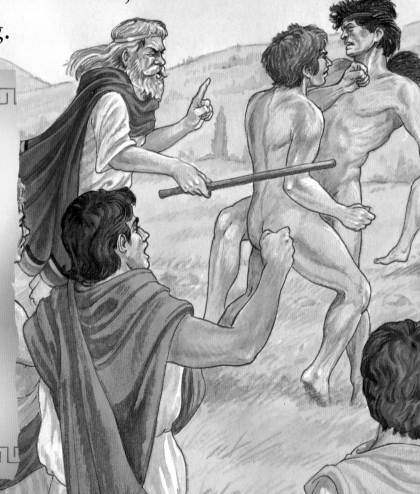

THE GREEKS HELD SPORTS contests to please their gods. The most important were the Olympic Games, held every four years in honour of Zeus. Athletes came from all over Greece to take part.

Only the fittest Greeks competed in the games, but almost everyone enjoyed sports for fun. Cities had both public and private gyms, where people could wrestle, run and practise their throwing.

Events at the games
Sports at the games included running, long jump, boxing, wrestling and chariot-racing. Athletes also threw the javelin or discus.

CAN YOU BELIEVE IT?
Only men took part in the Olympic Games.

YES. But women had their own games. They were held in honour of Hera, queen of the gods.

YOU MUST BE JOKING!

For most events at the games, the athletes were naked. However, there was one very difficult race that had to be run in full armour! It reminded everyone that the games were important training for soldiers.

PRIZE ATHLETE

Winning sportsmen were rewarded with beautiful crowns of olive leaves and ribbons to tie to their arms and legs. They also won jars of olive oil or wine, and reams of expensive cloth.

GREAT GREEKS

T**HERE WERE MANY CLEVER THINKERS** and scientists in Greece. They came up with new ideas by being curious when they looked at their world – and beyond. The names they gave the stars are still used today.

The Greek doctor Hippocrates made huge leaps in medicine. Before his time, people thought disease was a punishment from the gods. He showed them that diseases had natural causes.

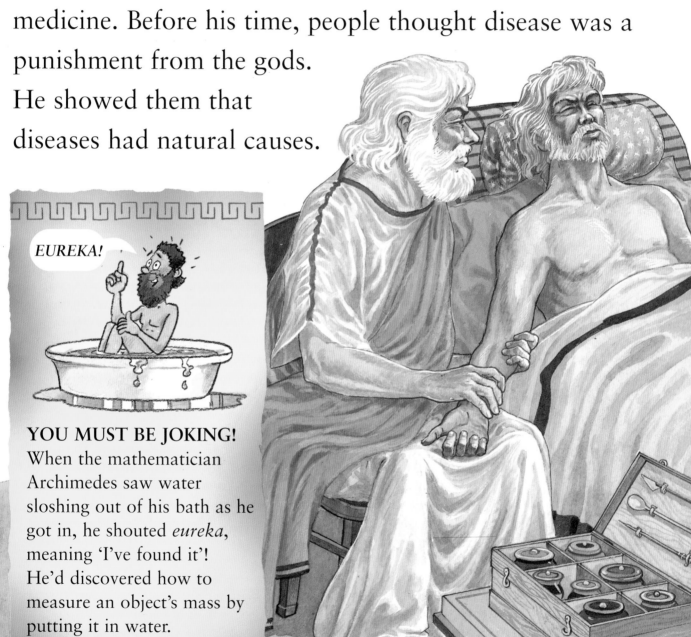

EUREKA!

YOU MUST BE JOKING!
When the mathematician Archimedes saw water sloshing out of his bath as he got in, he shouted *eureka*, meaning 'I've found it'! He'd discovered how to measure an object's mass by putting it in water.

CAN YOU BELIEVE IT?
The Greeks poisoned their best thinker.

YES. Socrates was one of the greatest Greek thinkers but not everyone liked his ideas. He was accused of inventing new gods and corrupting the young, and was forced to drink deadly hemlock.

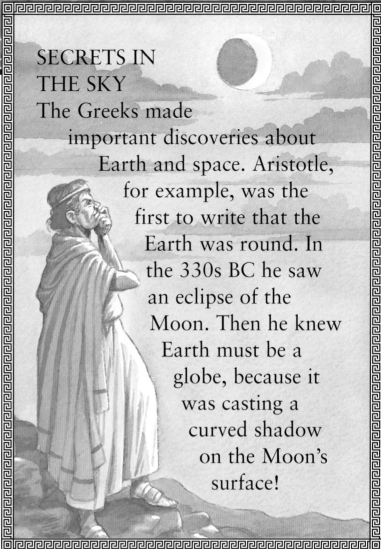

SECRETS IN THE SKY
The Greeks made important discoveries about Earth and space. Aristotle, for example, was the first to write that the Earth was round. In the 330s BC he saw an eclipse of the Moon. Then he knew Earth must be a globe, because it was casting a curved shadow on the Moon's surface!

Bedside manner
Greek doctors examined patients' bodies and asked questions in order to diagnose (work out) their disease.

END OF ANCIENT GREECE

THE AGE OF THE CITY STATES came to an end in the 300s BC. That was when Alexander, a powerful prince from Macedonia, fought to become ruler of them all. Alexander built up an empire that went beyond Greece into the Middle East and Egypt.

Greek power thrived for another century or so. Then, in 146 BC, the Roman army invaded mainland Greece. Soon, all of the ancient Greek world was part of the Roman empire. But even then, Greek culture and ideas lived on – because the Romans copied them!

Horseback warrior Alexander the Great was a superb soldier. He conquered Persia, Babylon and parts of ancient India.

YOU MUST BE JOKING!
The Romans nicked all the Greeks' gods! Once they controlled Greek lands, the Romans adopted the Greek gods. They gave them all new, Roman names – except Apollo who kept his old name!

THE ROMANS ARRIVE

After the death of Alexander, the different parts of Greece went back to their old quarrelsome ways. At first, the Romans tried to help sort out their differences. Then they grew impatient. It was easier just to capture all the Greek lands for themselves.

CAN YOU BELIEVE IT?
The Greeks conquered the ancient Egyptians.

YES. Alexander the Great built a new capital at Alexandria, with its own Greek-style lighthouse.

INDEX

Achilles 20
Aegean Sea 5
Aesclepius 24
Alexander the Great 30–31
Aphrodite 23
Apollo 17, 22, 25, 30
Archimedes 28
Ares 23
Argonauts 21
Aristotle 29
armies 4, 8–9, 27, 30, 31
Artemis 17, 23
Assembly 6–7
Athene 23
Athens 6, 7, 8, 23

baths 12
Black Sea 5
boats 4, 9
burglars 14

children 15, 16–17
city states 4, 6–7
clothing 12–13, 15
colonies 5
Crete 21
Cronos 23
Cyclops 21

Delphi 25

Demeter 22, 23
Dionysos 19, 22
doctors 28–29
drama 18–19

Egyptians 31
entertainment 11, 18–21
Euripides 20

festivals 24–25
food 10–11, 14, 24

gods 17, 19, 20, 22–23, 24–25, 30

Hades 22, 23
Hephaestos 23
Hera 23, 26
Hermes 22
Hesiod 20
Hestia 22, 23
Hippocrates 28
Homer 9
housing 14

Jason 21

Mediterranean Sea 5
Minotaur 20–21
mirrors 12
music 11, 19

Mycenae 7

Odysseus 21
olive oil 11, 12, 27
Olympic Games 26–27
Olympus, Mount 22
ostraka 7

Pan 22
Parthenon 23
Persephone 23
Poseidon 22

Romans 30, 31

schools 16–17
science 28–29
slaves 11, 15
Socrates 29
Sparta 6, 8, 9
sports 16, 26–27
Styx, River 20, 25

temples 23, 24–25
Theseus 20–21
trade 4–5
Trojan War 8–9, 21

water clock 6
wine 10, 19, 24, 27

Zeus 22, 23, 26